What others are saying about...
SURVIVING

Note: All three of these individuals experienced the roller coaster ride of divorce with their parents during the teen years.

"This book is a very helpful tool for both parents and children who are going through the difficult and life changing process of divorce. It personally gave me a sense of hopefulness and encouragement that I honestly did not expect. It assured me that what I was feeling was normal, okay, and part of the whole experience of coping and getting through the difficulty of the divorce."

- **Fain Watson** (parents divorce when she was 18)

"This book was very helpful to me because this time of year is always the hardest for me when it comes to the divorce. You did a very good job of being factual with out being uncaring about the situation."

- **Tristan Wheeler** (parents divorced when he was 16)

"*What an invaluable resource for any teen to have that is asking the how and why questions of their parents divorce. You just never understand the pain and confusion until it happens to your family. This book helps you to understand that you are truly not alone in what you are experiencing.*"

- **Jordan Vaughn** (parents divorced when he was 15)

SURVIVING

Helping Teens Find Peace
on the Roller Coaster Ride of Divorce.

JOE WELLS, M.Min.

KAIO PUBLICATIONS, INC.

First Published by Focus Press

Section 1: **INTRODUCTION**

Phil sits in his room, staring into nothingness, because that's what his life has just become – at least that's what he's feeling. His parents just told him they were divorcing after 20 years together. Why couldn't they just stop screaming at each other? Why did Dad have to work so much, and why did Mom put so much pressure on him at home? How could they do this to me? Did I do something to drive my parents apart? They said they loved me, but it doesn't feel like it.

Sarah comes home from a normal day at school, but what she finds at home is not normal in her world. Mom is sitting all alone in her room just looking out into thin air. Dad is not coming home tonight. Sarah doesn't understand. Why would Dad do this to us? Who is this other woman, and why would he do this to Mom? I hate him! I miss him and wish he were here! I don't understand. Why???

Chances are, you're reading this book because you know exactly what's going on in Phil's and Sarah's lives. You probably understand more than you would like. Your world may have crashed as your parents divorced, and you may be stuck in a terrible storm. You may be confused, angry or sad. Maybe you have had thoughts of suicide or just an all-around feeling of "nobody loves me." What will you do, and where can you turn?

Did you know you're not alone? There are teens all across America who are dealing with divorce just as you are. As a matter of fact, probably some of your friends at school or church have dealt with divorce – or are right now. Just like you, they know what it feels like to wonder what's going to happen now, or what my family will be like. The hurt, anger, fear and guilt have all visited them, too. You're not alone, but knowing that probably doesn't make it any easier right now, does it? In time it may, but for now, keep on reading. You might find a small nugget of gold that will help you in your situation.

Section 2: **IS WHAT I'M FEELING OK?**

STOP: Write down what you are feeling right now. No one will see this, so be honest.

_____

_____

Consider amusement parks. The huge roller coasters always have the longest lines, don't they? It seems everyone loves the rush of speed – the climb to the top along with the sudden drop to the bottom. Throw in the twists, turns and loops, and you've got a thrill ride that many will stand in line hours for.

If we're talking about roller coasters, then it's great; however, if we're talking about emotions and feelings, it's not much fun, is it?

When your parents go through a divorce, you might feel as if you're on a roller coaster, except it's not fun and you badly want to get off. You climb the initial hill of shock and sadness and then encounter the drop of hatred and rage. Then there's the sharp turn to the right of depression followed by the loop of uncertainty of what will happen next. The feeling of emptiness that eats away at your heart is, at times, just too much. The anger at one parent or both seems to be all you can think about. Looking around and seeing everyone else, in what seems like happy families, just makes it worse. You didn't ask to get on this ride. You weren't standing in line for it, but it happened. You were put here, and the deep desire to get off of it seems like it's out of your control.

So what do you do? How should you feel right now? There is no right or wrong answer to those questions. *One thing's for certain: you don't need someone telling you how to feel.* Each situation is different, and so is each teen that goes through it. You are handling it in your own way right now, and that's OK. No two people are the same; nor will they feel the same and act the same when it comes to this. However, what are some of the common emotions and feelings that most teens in your shoes go through? What about these:

Anger – It's easy to get mad sometimes, isn't it? Especially when something bad has been done to us. Many times in divorce, people get angry, and they show it in many ways. You might have seen your mom and dad shout at each other or even possibly throw something. You might have heard a door slam, or the wheels of the car squeal in the driveway as one of your parents peeled out.

We all get angry. Chances are, right now, you might be angry. Your anger might be directed at one of your parents. Maybe one of your parents walked out or cheated on the other. Or maybe you're mad at both of them. You might just be mad at the fact that your family is changing. What can you do with your anger?

That's a good question. What are your options? You could decide that since everything seems to be hitting you that you are going to hit back, literally. Your brothers or sisters could always be a target, but that would hurt someone who's already hurting and confused just like you. You could go to school and be the person who looks for a fight with every cross word or strange look, but that would only make people want to stay farther away from you and ultimately put you in detention.

Instead of lashing out with physical violence, you could just decide not to talk with anyone. After all, it was the people closest to you who hurt you, so why should you talk and trust anyone else, right? Well, if you do that, it will be very easy to slip into depression. That's where you just don't care about anything anymore. All of a sudden the sports you liked are not important, the band is not fun – even hanging out with your friends, which you used to love, will become not important. You could respond this way, but in truth, it will only bring you that much more hurt. You will want to be alone, but then you don't. It may not make much sense, but it's as if you want help, but you become quiet and hold back.

Although both of these are possible responses to the anger you might be feeling, neither of them is going to help you as much as 1) accepting that your anger is real, and 2) dealing with it by talking and writing about *why* you're angry.

Did you know being mad is not wrong? If it is, then we've got a problem, because Jesus seemed to get pretty mad when He entered the temple and used a whip to drive out those who were buying and selling items for sacrifice (John 2:13-17). It hurt Jesus that the people had begun using the temple, a place of prayer and worship, as a place of business. It was the disciples who remembered the writing from Psalm 69:9, "Zeal for Your house will consume Me" as they saw Jesus do this (NASB). So being angry about something is not wrong, but it does matter how you deal with your anger.

There are many ways you could deal with your anger, but let me remind you that the Bible tells us not to fall into sin when we are angry (Ephesians 4:26). That means being mad doesn't give you the right to hit someone or cuss them out. You shouldn't go out and destroy something, even though you might be feeling like it is only fair because you feel that your family is being destroyed. God doesn't want you to sit and let your anger just boil up inside of you like a pot of water on the stove, heating up until it boils over and causes a big mess. That's why in the same passage we read, "do not let the sun go down on your anger, and do not give the devil an opportunity" (NASB). There's something to be said for talking with your parents, a friend, preacher or counselor – or even writing out your anger instead of acting it out.

Rejection – Have you ever not been picked to play on a team in gym class? Or maybe you tried out for the band or play, but you were told they didn't need you for anything other than to clean the band room or work with the stage crew. Do you remember what it felt like the first time you heard your friends were getting together to play video games, but they didn't invite you to play? That feeling that we all hate, but we've all felt, is called rejection. It's when we feel left out or that we aren't good enough to be included. It hurts a lot, doesn't it?

Sometimes teens feel that their parents' divorce is a sign of one or both parents' turning their backs on them. It can really be a lonely place because you might think that your parents are so caught up in themselves that they aren't thinking about you. To be honest, that might be the case for some of you; however, those of you in that boat are the exception. Even if it seems that your parents are just thinking about themselves, that is likely not what is happening. They are hurting and are dealing with the divorce in their own way, but you are still their child, and they love you.

Did you know that Jesus understands what it means to be rejected? His own people turned their backs on Him when they handed Him over to be killed by the Romans. Can you imagine what Jesus would have felt as the Jewish leaders, those who were supposed to have been looking forward to Jesus coming to this earth, shouted "Crucify Him, crucify Him!"? You would think they would be the ones standing up for Him, but instead they were the ones shouting for Pilate to kill Him.

What about when Peter said he didn't know who Jesus was? Not only did he first tell Jesus, "Even if I have to die with You, I will not deny You" (Matthew 26:35, NASB), but he said he didn't know Jesus three times in one night. As soon as Peter did this, as Luke 22:61 tells us, Jesus turned and His eyes meet the eyes of Peter. Can you imagine that look? Talk about feeling rejected. Even though the rest of the world had turned their backs on Him, surely Jesus could count on those closest to Him here on this earth, right? No, He could not. He was alone.

That's the part of feeling rejected that hurts so much, isn't it? There are times when we can feel alone even though we have people all around, and divorce tends to be one of those times. As your family changes, you might feel very lonely. If you have brothers or sisters, they might be going through the same things. They might need to talk to you, or you might need to talk to them. You will learn that others are hurting just as you are. Lean on them. It's OK for you to tell them what you're feeling. It might surprise you to find out they are feeling some of the same things.

> **WRITE In your journal:** Write a note to yourself about what you're feeling and why.

Section 3: IT'S NOT YOUR FAULT

The date was October 25, 1986, and the Boston Red Sox faced the New York Mets in Game 6 of the World Series. The Red Sox were leading the series three games to two and only had to win one more to be crowned World Champions. The game entered extra innings, and the Sox had a two-run lead with two outs in the bottom of the 10th inning. New York came back to tie the game with three straight singles and a wild pitch. With the winning run in scoring position, Mookie Wilson hit a ground ball toward first base, where Bill Buckner was in position. The ball rolled right under Buckner's glove, through his legs and into right field. The runner scored and the Mets won, forcing Game 7. The Mets would go on to win that game, too, becoming World Champions.

Whose fault was that? Many in the sports world blamed Buckner. The ball was not hit that hard, and he was in position to make the play just as he had done countless times before. He must have felt horrible. Could you imagine feeling as if you had let down your teammates, your city, your fans? The world was screaming at Buckner and yelling, "It's your fault!"

Sometimes when parents divorce, some teens get this feeling. You might be one of those teens who think you could have done something to help, or at least not cause as much stress and problems. You might think to yourself, "If I had only not talked back as much" or "I should have done better in school and this would not be happening." The reality is that, deep down, parents understand what being a teen is all about. Your parents were both teens once, and they know that being a teen is part of growing up. We aren't always going to do everything perfect. Our parents know that, and no matter how much you think you could have done to make your parents' marriage better, the truth is it was not up to you. Their decisions are on them, and you are not to blame. Did you get that? *It's not your fault!*

> **WRITE In your journal:** Have there been times in your life that you feel you've caused your family stress? What are some of these times, and what are some things you wish you could have done different? Now beside all of these write, "I Did Not Cause The Divorce".

Stress hits every family. It might be money problems, work problems, house problems or, yes, family problems. Usually there's more than one issue that causes a major issue like divorce to happen. Sometimes parents don't agree on what to do about certain things like money and raising the children. Sometimes one parent decides he or she needs to go outside of the marriage to meet a need that should have been met within the marriage. Whatever the situation, problems happen, and blame begins to be placed. You might be feeling very strongly that one of your parents is to blame for the entire mess. Maybe it's your dad, maybe it's your mom. Maybe one left and the other parent is carrying the responsibility of raising you and your brothers and sisters all alone. Before the blame gets laid at the feet of your dad or mom, let me tell you about a friend.

I first met this young man when he was a senior in high school. His parents had been divorced for some time, but every time we talked, it was clear he was struggling with his relationship with his father. There's always a lot of blame to go around, and in this case, much of it appeared to be on his dad.

This young man grew up and got married, and now he has his own child. As he looks back at the whole situation, he says he can see the bigger picture. He sees some things that both parents might have done that made their marriage difficult and resulted in the divorce. "Don't be too quick to place blame" was his advice when it came to this issue.

So what's the point, you might ask? Are you ready for the secret? Here goes…none of us are perfect. I know – big surprise. But it's a point that might help you in dealing with some of what is going through your mind right now. Once you realize that you are not to blame for your parents' divorce, you might be tempted to place the blame somewhere. That is only natural; however, as you begin to come to an understanding about everything that took place, let me encourage you to remember how God forgives.

It is our sin that separates all of us from God. Your sin might be different than that of the person sitting next to you in homeroom, but the Bible makes it very clear that "all have sinned and fall short" (Romans 3:23). As a result of our sins, we deserve death (Romans 6:23), but it was God Who planned to forgive us and allow us back into a relationship with Him. As a matter of fact, He sent Jesus to die for the people of the world when we were "helpless," "ungodly," "sinners" and "enemies" of God (Romans 5:6-10). For those who obey the Gospel, Jesus takes their blame of sin, and God forgives completely even though they don't deserve it. Now that would be hard to do!

STOP:
1) Do you feel your parents' divorce is your fault? Why do you think this? _____
_____
_____

2) Who do you blame right now for the divorce? Write out why you feel this way. _____
_____
_____

3) Which is easier: To Place Blame or To Forgive? Why do you think that is the case?
_____
_____
_____

Section 4: HOW WILL THIS CHANGE MY LIFE

WRITE In your journal: Are you afraid of how this divorce will change your life? What are your fears and concerns?

Let's return to Sarah and Phil.

Sarah has practiced so hard for this night. The volleyball team is geared up for the district championship, and she knows this night will be something to remember for a long time. But for some reason, her mind is somewhere else. It's in the stands, wondering how things will be tonight when both of her parents show up to watch. They've been divorced now for three months, and the way they talk about each other only fuels the fire of uncertainty. She thinks to herself, "How will it be when they see each other? Will they sit beside each other or even near each other? Will they speak, and if they do, will they at least be nice to each other? I hope they don't embarrass me."

Phil walks through the only house he has known for the past 15 years.

He notices in the hallway there are a lot of empty nails where pictures used to hang. As he walks into the living room, he glances up at the bookshelf and notices how empty they are. Dad's books are all gone, along with his favorite picture from last summer with his whole family in it. He sits down, leaving the TV off, and just notices how many small things have changed. His stomach begins to hurt as the pain of what has happened returns. As memories run through his mind from holidays and special moments from the past, he can only cry and wonder why and what's next.

You might not be in the same place as Sarah and Phil, but chances are you've asked yourself how things will change. You might be in a home that is too expensive to live in with only one parent working, so you might have to move. If you move, will you have to move schools and make new friends? What about spending time with each parent individually? You might wonder how that will work – and if it will work.

Change is part of being on that roller coaster discussed earlier. You know it's coming; you didn't sign up for it, but you have to deal with it. Change will happen, and some of it might be very difficult for you, but that doesn't mean you can't find the good in your situation. You might find that your relationship with your parents gets better. If one parent had not been really involved in your life, you might see that parent trying to be more involved. You may become very tight with your brothers and sisters as you are forced to help each other and care for each other a little more than you did before. You might even find that your parents are a little happier because whatever stress they were feeling is gone.

In focusing on the good that you can find in this bad, make sure you remember that with any change there are going to be times of difficulty. You might actually have to move into another house. Maybe you will stay in the same school, but you might not be that lucky. The holidays are going to be different now as you have to share time at two different houses. Those special events that come up in your life might be a little weird.

The best way to handle this change is to talk to your parents. Let them know what you're thinking and what you're afraid off. It's OK to be afraid and have some doubts and concerns. Just let them know about them so that you are not trying to deal with them all on your own. Chances are, they might have some of the same concerns you do, and by talking about it, you can help them and they can help you.

In all things, remember that even when it doesn't seem like it, God is still in control. Regardless of what changes come your way and when they may happen, know that He is always there and will always be in the same place, loving you. It was King David who wrote, "In peace I will both lie down and sleep, for You alone, O Lord, make me to dwell in safety" (Psalm 4:8). No matter what happened to David, he was at peace as he put his trust in God. You can have that peace tonight as well if you will do the same.

STOP: What are some of the things you need to talk to your parents about? _____
_____
_____

Section 5: WHAT DO I DO NOW?

Reality sets in. Life has changed, and it will never be the same. You're on the roller coaster, and the ride is not slowing down. What do you do? Once you get to the point of being able to look ahead, consider the following suggestions.

1) *Get closer to God than you have been.*

This is first because there are going to be some hard days ahead. That's not to scare you, but to let you know they're coming. How will you handle them when they do? That's easy to answer when you consider the account of David and Goliath from I Samuel 17. Do you remember how Goliath was causing the entire Israelite army to be afraid? David heard him insulting God one day and responded by marching out to meet the giant. He had one sling and five smooth stones, which in the hands of someone who knew how to use them would be very dangerous. But it's what David said to Goliath that is so strong. He said, "This day the Lord will deliver you up into my hands, and I will strike you down…" (I Samuel 17:46) There was no worry or doubt in the voice of David. He was sure what was going to happen.

In your life, a Goliath will come after you. If you haven't spent time developing your faith by spending time in reading your Bible and putting what you read into practice or in serious prayer to God, then you probably won't be able to respond with the same faith as David did. However, once you draw closer to God, the Bible says He will draw near to you (James 4:8).

2) Don't change too much too fast.

Let's face it: there are times when you think that nobody is caring for you. I know that might sound bad, but with what has taken place between your mom and dad, it might be easy for you to slip into feeling that they are wrapped up in their own worlds and aren't paying attention to you. You might be in the middle of a sports season or preparing for that big concert. It might be that you have a major project due at school and could really use some help, but you know so much is going on with the divorce that you don't want to add any stress.

You might be feeling like pulling back from some of the activities you are involved in right now. Don't! You might have to if you move to a different community, but understand this: as difficult as things are right now, you don't want to change too much at one time because that will only add to the stress and your feelings that nobody cares. If you enjoy playing football, keep playing. If your sport is soccer, then remember that it's good for you to stay as involved with what interest you. It might be that you like hanging out with your friends or going to the mall. Whatever it is, try to stay involved even when you don't feel like it. You'll be glad you did.

3) Let others support you.

Have you ever gone rock climbing, when you'd have to wear the harness with the rope through it to catch you if you fell? I have a couple times, and each time there was a partner with me to make sure I didn't fall. He helped me along the way as I tried to find the best way up the rock. If I slipped and fell, he was there to hold the rope so my harness would lock and hold me. The thought of falling always made the hair on the back of my neck stand up as I pictured what it would be like to tumble or just drop down; however, my trust in the person who was helping me through the task made it easier to keep going.

Right now you're on that rock. You are climbing, but sometimes it gets hard to see where to put your hand next or what step to take so that you will have a good place to push up. You might get tired of climbing or even be afraid of slipping and falling. You think about how bad things are, how tired you are, or maybe even how big the task is. Can you do it? Yes, you can, and having people there with you to catch you when you fall, to help direct you when you can't see the next hand hold or foot placement makes it that much easier. It's still up to you to climb, but it helps knowing someone else is there with you along the way.

4) Work on forgiving those who let you down.

How do you forgive when it feels like your entire world has been rocked because of a divorce? There might be so much anger and fear inside of you right now that you don't know what to do. The roller coaster is roaring, and you want off more than you've ever wanted anything. Maybe you want things to return to the way they were when you were younger, to a time when you had good memories of holidays and birthdays. Your life has changed, and it hurts badly. Sometimes it can be very hard to forgive the people responsible for that change.

God understands forgiving those who have done something wrong against you. To show just how bad it was, He told Hosea, a prophet of Israel, to go and marry a prostitute and have children with her. This marriage to Gomer (I know, I thought the same thing!) was to be an example to the people of just how much they had let God down by being unfaithful to Him, but also to show that, even though they had not loved God and treated Him right, He still loved them. Even though the armies from Assyria were going to come in and attack the Israelites (Hosea 10:6), God was not going to allow them to be destroyed. He loved them and gave them a chance to come back to Him, even though they didn't deserve it.

We have the same love from God that He gave the Israelites in Hosea's day. We read that Jesus came to the earth and died on the cross – not because we deserved it, but rather because He loved us before we loved Him (Romans 5:6-10; I John 4:15). That's the story of the cross: God's showing His love by sending His Son, Jesus, to die a very cruel death so that we could be forgiven for hurting God with our sin.

Do those who've hurt you deserve forgiveness? Maybe not, but your hurt won't go away until you can reach that point of forgiving them anyway. That doesn't mean that you have to accept what was done as OK. It does mean that just as God forgives us, we need to be able to completely forgive those who do wrong to us. Healing will happen when you learn to forgive those who have done you wrong.

Section 6: THE RIDE OF A LIFETIME

Consider the rush you experience while getting off a totally amazing ride. Your blood is pumping and your legs are weak. Your hair looks like an airplane just buzzed you, and your lips are dry from the blast of the air.

If you have friends with you, you discuss the best part and scariest parts as you run to see the photo of what you looked like on the ride. If you feel like overpaying for the picture, you take the picture home with you so you can always remember that day, that ride and that feeling.

Divorce is ugly and not easy. There's always hurt and change, but one day you'll get to the point of looking back at yourself on this roller coaster. Your hair will be windblown and your legs might be a little different. You'll remember the twists and the turns, the ups and the downs, but there will be a day when you look back and see who you've become since the ride of a lifetime. You didn't choose to get on the ride, but you had to hold on. There were times you wanted off so badly that that's all you could think about, but when you look back, you will understand the growth that has taken place.

Did you know that some teens say their relationship with their parents got better since their parents' divorce? Their parents actually spend more time with them now, hanging out and trying to get to know and understand them in ways they didn't before the divorce. Some teens say they grew and are better able to care for others who are hurting and that they feel more compassion now than they did before. Others will say they became better problem solvers and better listeners through the whole process. They grew for the better even through difficult times.

No one expects you to be there today. What you are going through is very real and painful, and it's OK for you to take your time as you struggle through these very difficult days. Also, let me remind you this doesn't have to define who you are nor what your relationship with your spouse will be like in the future. Look at what the Bible teaches on marriage / divorce (Matthew 19: 1-12; I Corinthians 7). The notes you wrote yourself in the journal pages and the time you spent answering the questions will always be something you can come back to and help you remember your journey. Just remember, God loves you more than anyone else on this earth, and He understands what you're going through.

WRITE In your journal: Looking ahead, write in your journal what you want for your family from this moment on. Be specific about your goals. Then write out your prayer to God as you ask Him to help your family in the future.

He who dwells in the shelter of the Most
High will abide in the shadow of the Almighty.
I will say to the LORD, "My refuge and my fortress,
my God, in whom I trust."
For he will deliver you from the snare of
the fowler and from the deadly pestilence.
He will cover you with his pinions, and under
his wings you will find refuge;
his faithfulness is a shield and buckler.
You will not fear the terror of the night,
nor the arrow that flies by day,
nor the pestilence that stalks in darkness,
nor the destruction that wastes at noonday.
A thousand may fall at your side, ten thousand at
your right hand, but it will not come near you.
You will only look with your eyes and see the
recompense of the wicked.
Because you have made the LORD your dwelling
place-- the Most High, who is my refuge.

(Psalm 91:1-9, ESV)

Maccoby, E., & Mnookin, R. H. (1992). *Dividing the child: Social and legal dilemmas of custody.* Cambridge, MA: Harvard University Press.

Wallerstein, J. S., Lewis, J., & Blakeslee, S. (2000). *The unexpected legacy of divorce: The 25 year landmark study.* New York: Hyperion.

My Journal

www.ingramcontent.com/pod-product-compliance
Lightning Source LLC
Chambersburg PA
CBHW050451010526
44118CB00013B/1784